peaceful classical
piano solos

a collection of 30 pieces

ISBN: 978-1-70514-011-6

Visit Hal Leonard Online at
www.halleonard.com

Contact Us:
Hal Leonard
7777 West Bluemound Road
Milwaukee, WI 53213
Email: info@halleonard.com

In Europe contact:
Hal Leonard Europe Limited
42 Wigmore Street
Marylebone, London, W1U 2RN
Email: info@halleonardeurope.com

In Australia contact:
Hal Leonard Australia Pty. Ltd.
4 Lentara Court
Cheltenham, Victoria, 3192 Australia
Email: info@halleonard.com.au

Adagietto

from *Symphony No. 5 in C-sharp minor*

By Gustav Mahler

5

Adagio sostenuto

from *Piano Sonata No. 14 in C-sharp minor, 'Moonlight Sonata'*

By Ludwig van Beethoven

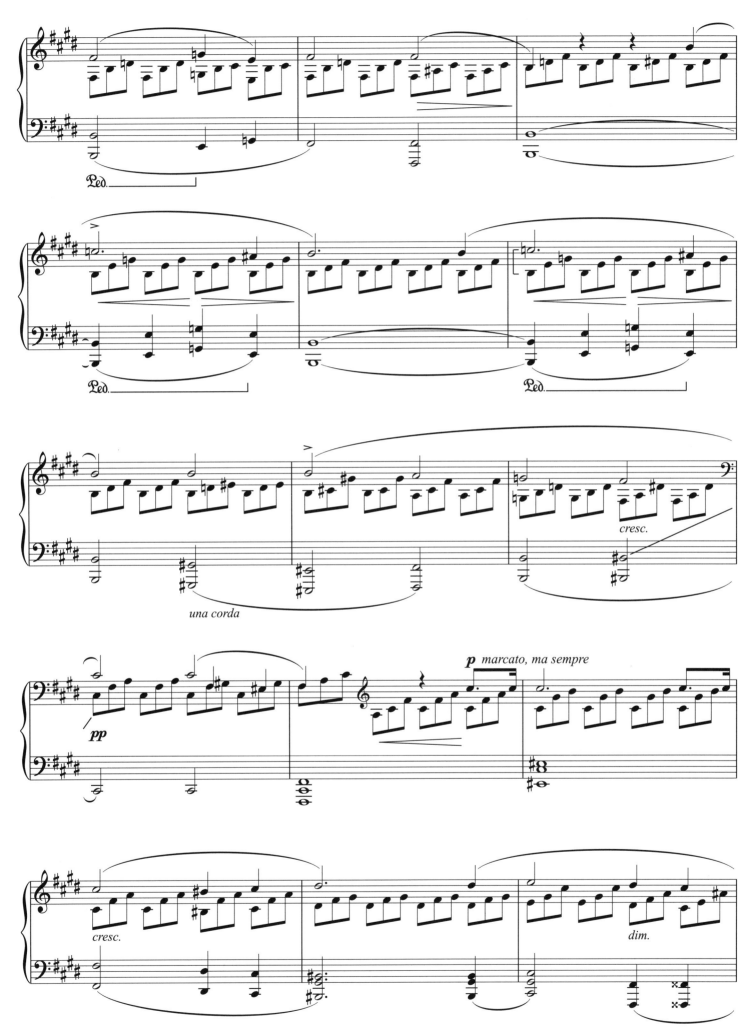

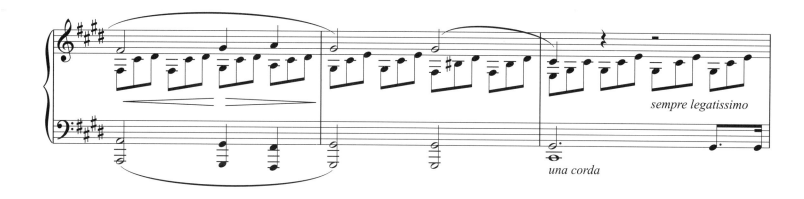

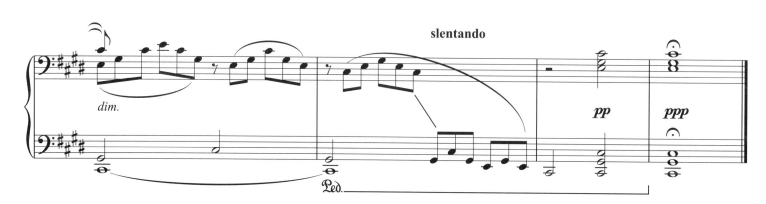

Andante

from *'Three-fours' Valse Suite, Op. 71*

By Samuel Coleridge-Taylor

Ave Maria, D. 839

By Franz Schubert

Andante con moto

from *Lieder ohne Worte, Op. 19b*

By Felix Mendelssohn

Canción

from *Obras desconocidas*

By Manuel de Falla

Clair de Lune

from *Suite bergamasque, L. 75*

By Claude Debussy

Andante très expressif ♩. = 52

Dreaming

from *4 Sketches, Op. 15*

By Amy Marcy Beach

Gymnopédie No. 1

By Erik Satie

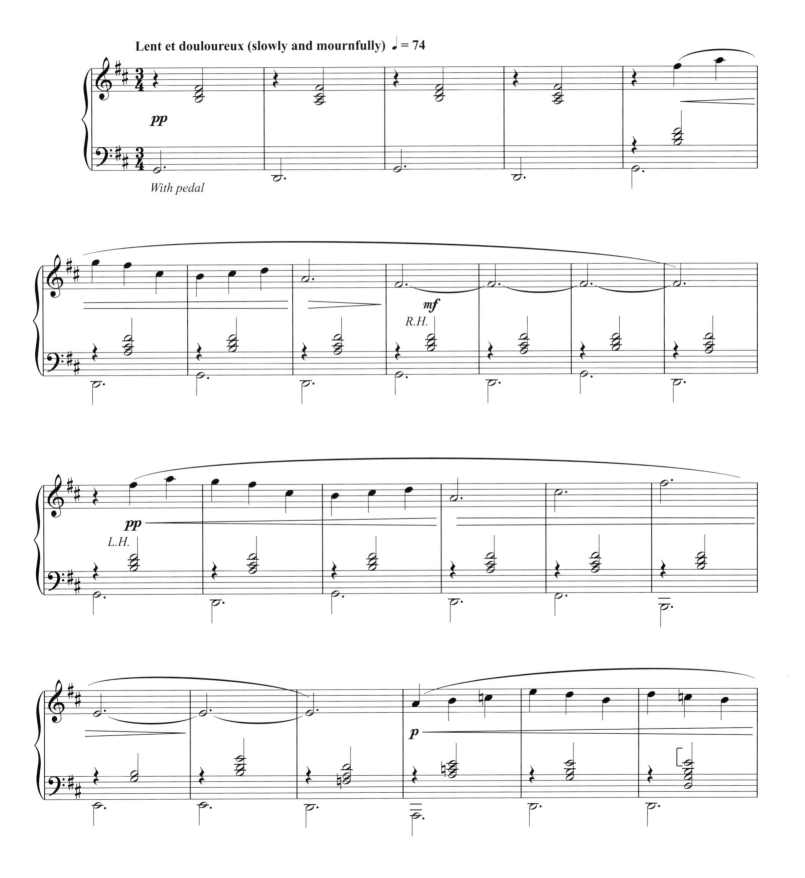

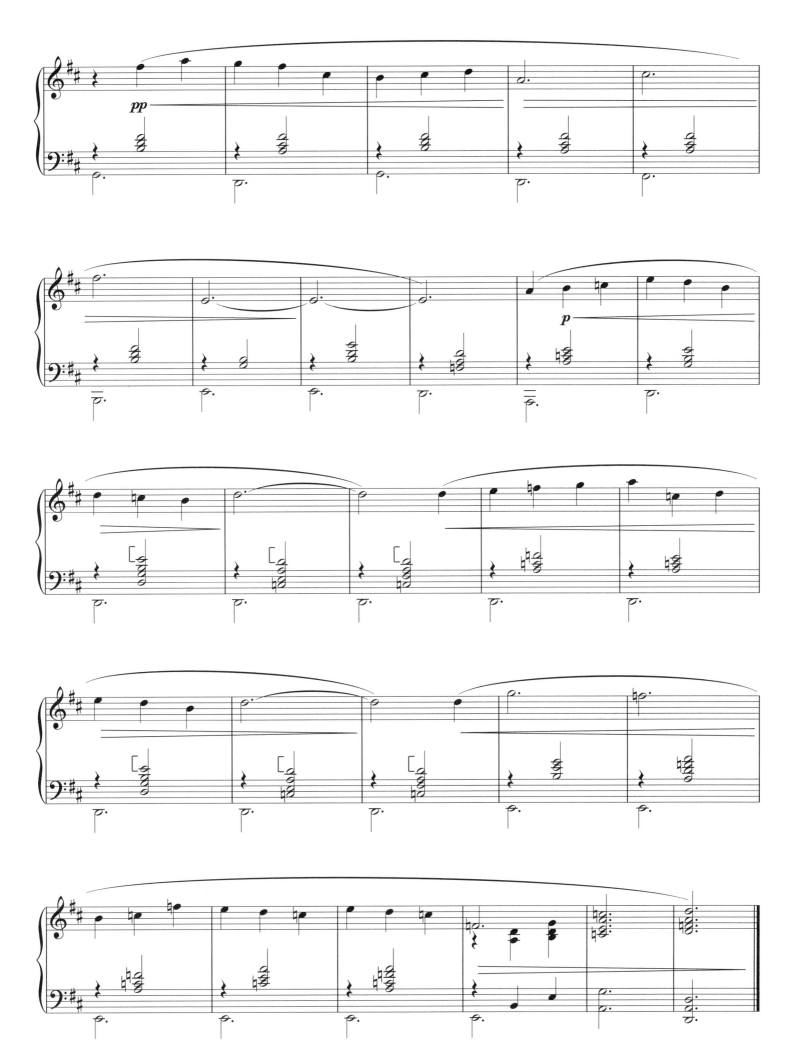

Intermezzo

from *Cavalleria Rusticana*

By Pietro Mascagni

Largo

from *The Four Seasons, 'Winter'*

By Antonio Vivaldi

Largo "Ombra mai fu"

from *Xerxes, HWV 40*

By George Frideric Handel

Le Cygne (The Swan)

from *Le Carnaval des Animaux, R. 125*

By Camille Saint-Saëns

Lento appassionato

from *6 Mélodies pour le piano, Op. 4 & 5*

By Fanny Mendelssohn

Largo Theme

from *Symphony No. 9 in E Minor, Op. 95, 'From the New World'*

By Antonín Dvořák

Liebesträum No. 3 in A flat

By Franz Liszt

poco cresc. ed agitato

p

p più animato con passione

Love Theme

from *Romeo and Juliet TH. 42*

By Pyotr Il'yich Tchaikovsky

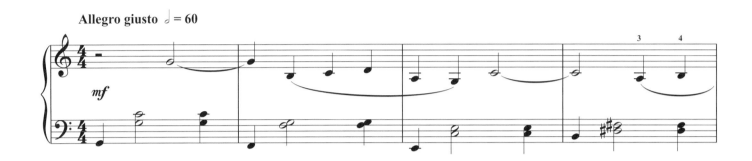

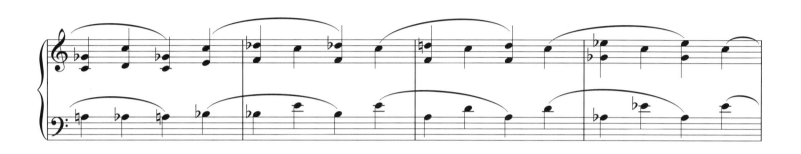

Morning Mood

from *Peer Gynt, Op. 23*

By Edvard Grieg

Méditation

from *Thaïs*

By Jules Massenet

Nimrod

from *Variations on an Original Theme, Op. 36, 'Enigma'*

By Edward Elgar

Nocturne in E-flat Major, Op. 9, No. 2

By Frédéric Chopin

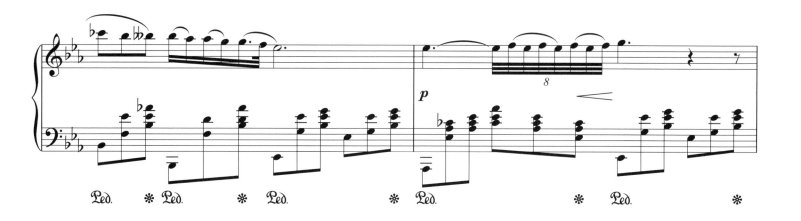

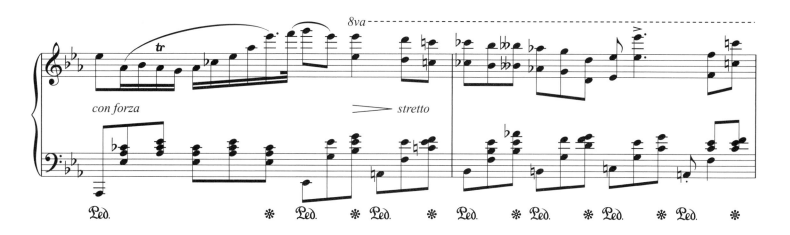

Pavane pour une infante défunte

By Maurice Ravel

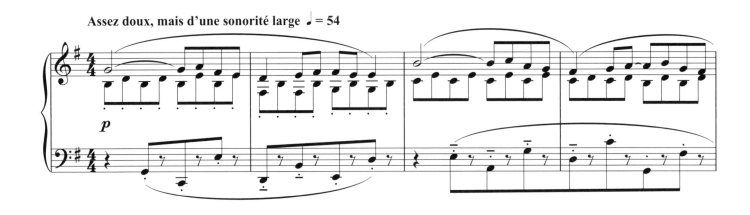

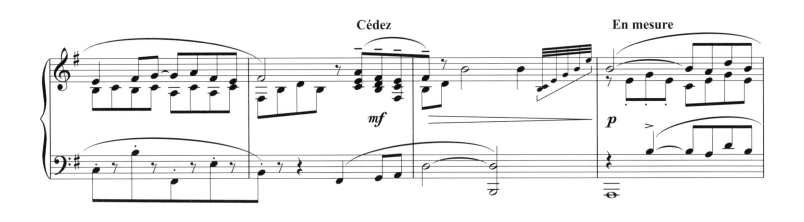

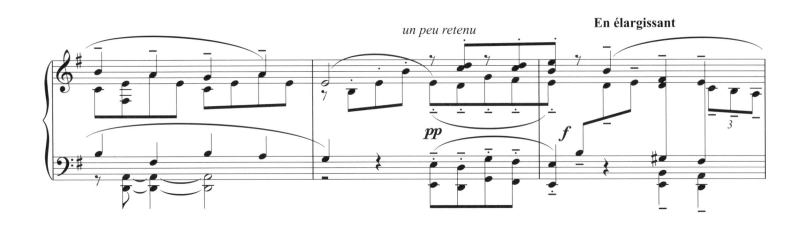

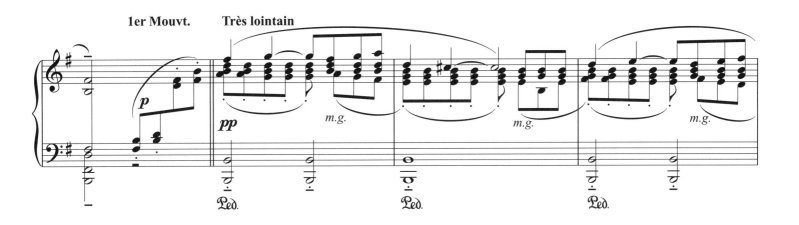

1er Mouvt.   Très lointain

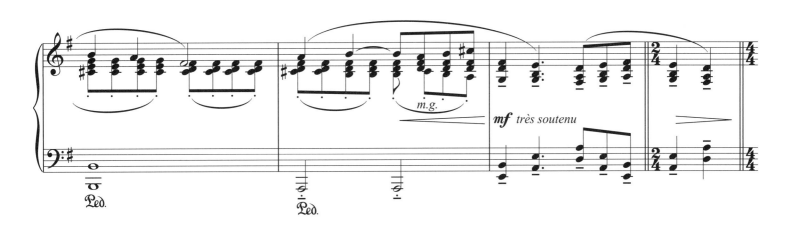

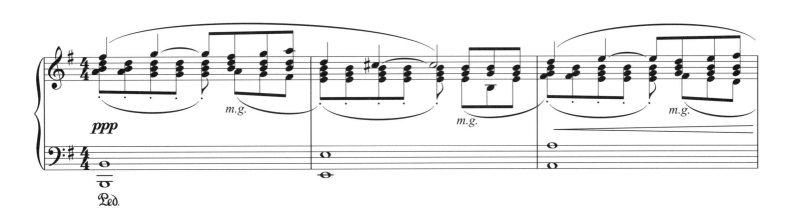

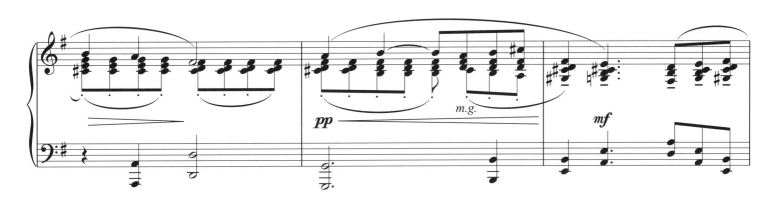

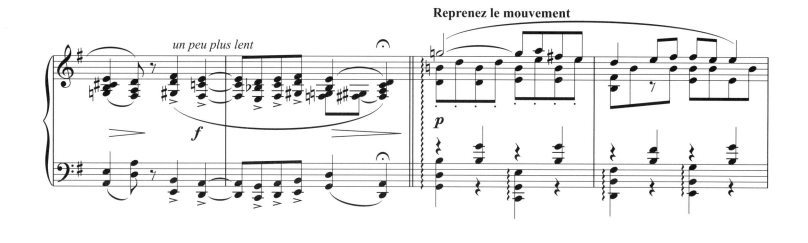

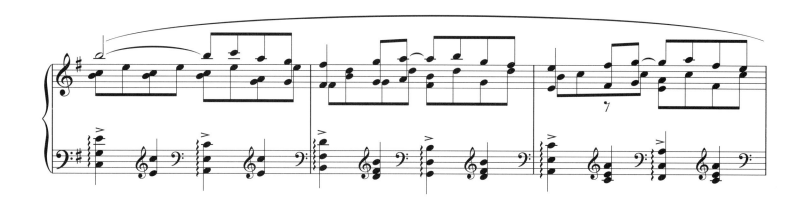

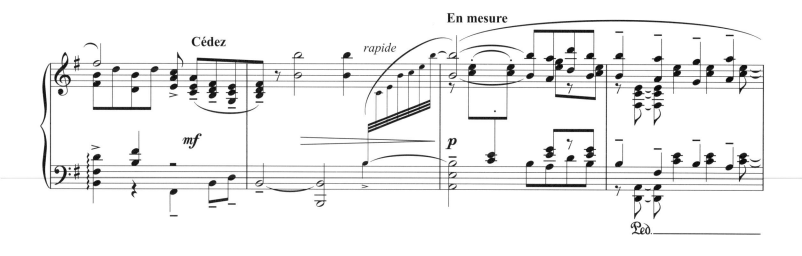

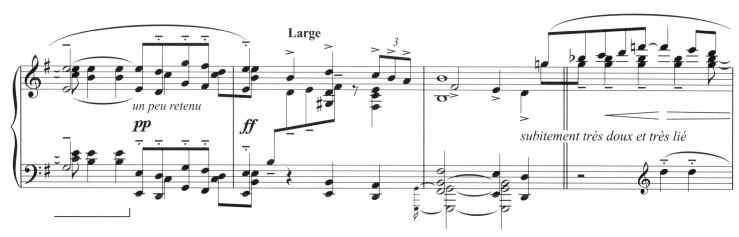

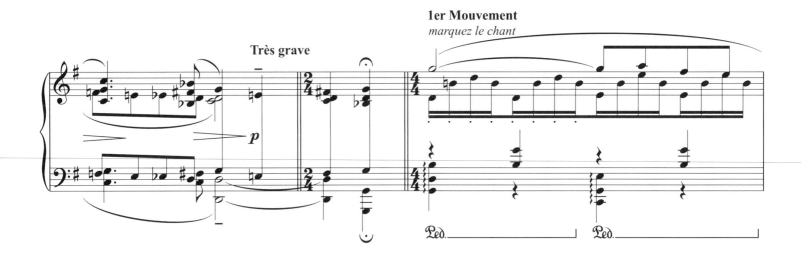

1er Mouvement
marquez le chant

Très grave

sim.

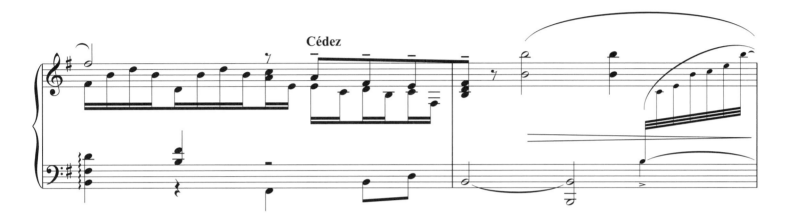

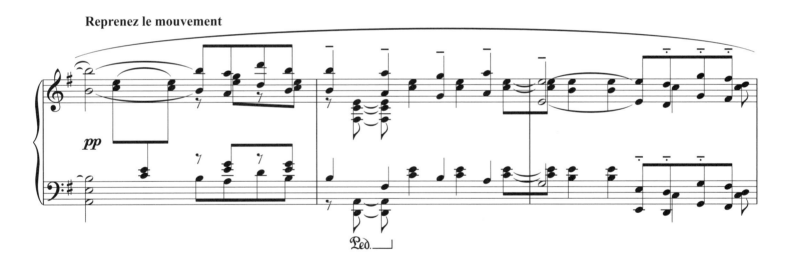

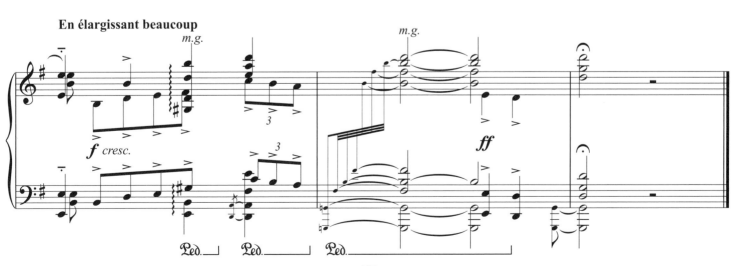

Pie Jesu

from *Requiem, Op. 48*

By Gabriel Fauré

Prelude in C Major

from *The Well-Tempered Clavier, Book 1, BWV 846*

By Johann Sebastian Bach

Panis Angelicus

By César Franck

Romance

from *Eine Kleine Nachtmusik, K. 525*

By Wolfgang Amadeus Mozart

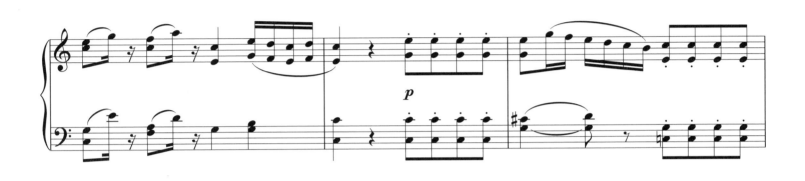

To a Wild Rose

from *Ten Woodland Sketches, Op. 51*

By Edward MacDowell

Träumerei

from *Kinderszenen, Op. 15*

By Robert Schumann

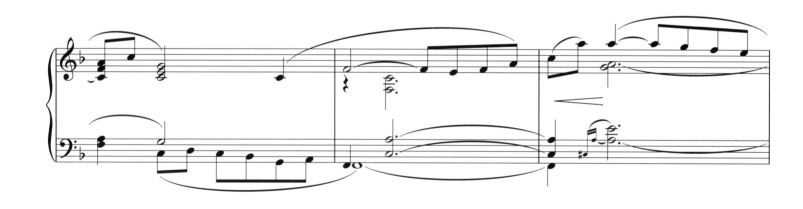

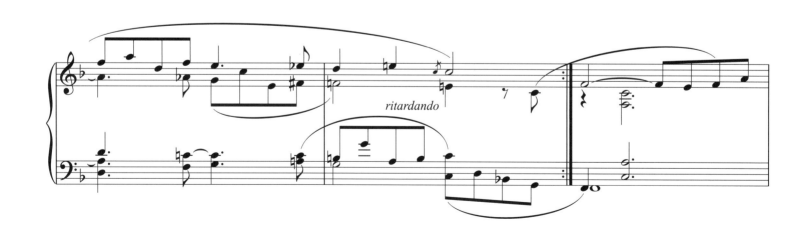

Warum willst du and're fragen

from *12 Gedichte aus Liebesfrühling, Op. 37*

Words by Friedrich Rückert
Music by Clara Schumann

Wiegenlied (Lullaby)

from *5 Lieder, Op. 49*

By Johannes Brahms

dim. e rall. al fine

Discover the rest of the series...

ORDER No. HL00286009

ORDER No. HL00286428

ORDER No. HL00334969

ORDER No. HL00295379

Just visit your local music shop and ask to see our huge range of music in print.

www.halleonard.com